Read & Resp[...]

Ages 7–11

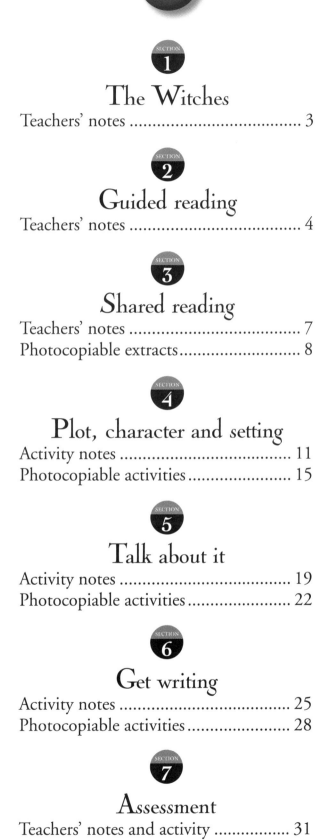

SECTION 1

The Witches

Teachers' notes 3

SECTION 2

Guided reading

Teachers' notes 4

SECTION 3

Shared reading

Teachers' notes 7
Photocopiable extracts........................... 8

SECTION 4

Plot, character and setting

Activity notes 11
Photocopiable activities...................... 15

SECTION 5

Talk about it

Activity notes 19
Photocopiable activities...................... 22

SECTION 6

Get writing

Activity notes 25
Photocopiable activities...................... 28

SECTION 7

Assessment

Teachers' notes and activity 31
Photocopiable activity 32

Read & Respond

Ages 7–11

Author: Jillian Powell

Commissioning Editor: Rachel Mackinnon

Editor: Roanne Charles

Assistant Editor: Jo Kemp

Series Designer: Anna Oliwa

Designer: Dan Prescott

Text © 2011 Jillian Powell © 2011 Scholastic Ltd

Designed using Adobe InDesign

Published by Scholastic Ltd,
Book End, Range Road, Witney,
Oxfordshire OX29 0YD
www.scholastic.co.uk

Printed by Bell & Bain
1 2 3 4 5 6 7 8 9   1 2 3 4 5 6 7 8 9 0

British Library Cataloguing-in-Publication Data
A catalogue record for this book is available from the British Library.

ISBN 978-1407-12708-8

Acknowledgements

The publishers gratefully acknowledge permission to reproduce the following copyright material: **AP Watt** for the use of illustrations from *The Witches* by Roald Dahl, illustrated by Quentin Blake. Illustrations © 1983, Quentin Blake. (1983, Jonathan Cape Ltd).
David Higham Associates for the use of extracts from *The Witches* by Roald Dahl. Text © 1983, Roald Dahl Nominee Ltd. (1983, Jonathan Cape Ltd).
Penguin Books Ltd for the use of the cover from *The Witches* by Roald Dahl. (1983, Jonathan Cape Ltd).
Every effort has been made to trace copyright holders for the works reproduced in this book, and the publishers apologise for any inadvertent omissions.

The Witches

About the book

First published in 1983, this enduring tale tells of a young boy, orphaned when his parents die in a car crash, who goes to live with his eccentric, cigar-smoking Norwegian grandmother, a grand storyteller and something of a witch expert. To help her recover from pneumonia, the pair go on holiday to Bournemouth, staying in a hotel where the witches of England are holding their annual convention, disguised as a branch of the RSPCC. Boy overhears The Grand High Witch Of All The World hatching a plot to get rid of all the children of England by turning them into mice, but before he can tell his grandmother, he is discovered by the witches and turned into a mouse. Between them, Boy and his grandmother concoct a plan to turn the witches' spell back on themselves, and so rid the world of witches.

At the heart of the story is the bond between Boy and his grandmother, unbroken even by his transformation into a mouse. Some classic fairytale themes – the small and weak outwitting the strong and powerful, good triumphing over evil, and poetic revenge or nemesis – are framed in a romping tale in which childish fears of ghouls and witches are faced head-on, with the author's famous delight in black comedy and the macabre.

About the author

Roald Dahl was born to Norwegian parents in Llandaff, Wales in 1916. Throughout his childhood and adolescence, he spent his summer holidays with his mother's family in Norway. Growing up, he loved stories and books, and his mother – 'a great teller of tales' – would sit and tell her children stories of trolls and other fantastical creatures. She is said to have been the inspiration for the grandmother in *The Witches*. At school, the young Dahl was good at sport, but his English teacher wrote that he was 'a persistent muddler' and 'incapable of marshalling his thoughts on paper.' Dahl related the story of his childhood and unhappy schooling in his autobiography *Boy: Tales of Childhood*.

He was an RAF pilot during the Second World War, but was shot down and eventually invalided out. His first published work, 'Shot Down Over Libya', was an account of his wartime experiences. In 1943, he wrote his first story for children about some mischievous mythical creatures, 'The Gremlins', also inspired by his time in the RAF.

By the 1960s, he was married and living with his wife and children in Buckinghamshire, where he wrote in a hut at the bottom of his garden. He became famous for often macabre short stories, with a twist at the end, and, increasingly, for his books for children, which were often controversial with their unflinching storylines and dark humour.

His children's books, most of them illustrated by Quentin Blake, have been translated into around 50 languages, and over a million copies are sold in the UK each year. Roald Dahl died in 1990 at the age of 74.

Facts and figures

The Witches was first published in 1983, when it won the Whitbread Award for Children's Books and the Federation of Children's Book Groups Award. It was adapted as a film in 1990 and as a stage play in 1992.

Guided reading

Expectations

Look at the front cover of *The Witches*. What clues does it give to the story inside? Ideas might vary depending on the edition, but note for instance: a little boy confronted by a pair of hideous clawed hands; a mouse with a bottle of blue, perhaps magic potion; a chaotic dining room scene of mice and witches; and an alarm clock, suggesting some sort of deadline.

Ask the children to tell you what they know about the author Roald Dahl and about any other books by him (or refer to other Dahl books read in class). What would they expect a book of his to be like? (Funny, rude, exciting, sometimes scary or a bit gruesome?)

Next, read the back cover blurb and the character list in the banner. What more do we learn about the story? (Its characters include a boy and his grandmother who are going to take on a coven of vile witches, led by The Grand High Witch, who want to *squish* all children.)

Finally, scan through the chapter headings and ask the children what they think the story will be like. (Dramatic, frightening, magical, fantasy?) If any children already know the story through reading the book or seeing the stage play or film, stress the importance of not spoiling the story for others.

'A Note about Witches' to 'The Grand High Witch'

Read the first chapter. Female teachers may want to 'play up' to Dahl's suggestion that they could be a witch in disguise! Ask the children whether this story is going to be realistic or fantasy. (A mixture of both.) How is the author being mischievous? (He raises questions in children's minds about women they know, including teachers.)

Read the next two chapters. Ask the children to summarise why witches are so dangerous. (They hate children and want to kill them, and are clever and can smell them out.) What is left unanswered at the end of this section? (What the witches did to Grandmamma and how she lost her thumb.)

Continue reading to the end of 'The Grand High Witch'. Pause to ask the children what more we learn about witches (how they cunningly transform children into creatures that ordinary people might kill) and what has happened in Boy's life (he has moved back to England and seen his first witch). Note the foreshadowing in the last sentence indicating that Boy is going to encounter more witches.

'Summer Holidays' to 'Frizzled Like a Fritter'

Read on through the next chapter. Ask the children what has happened to change the course of events. (Grandmamma has become ill so they are holidaying in England instead of Norway.) Speculate on what might be about to happen, given the earlier plot clue that witches book into hotels for their annual meetings disguised as other groups.

Read the next chapter and note the sustained tension in the risk that Boy might be sniffed out by the witches. What does The Grand High Witch's *frizzling* punishment warn us as well as Boy? (That she has the magic power to kill instantly.)

'Formula 86…' to 'Bruno'

Read the next two chapters. Ask a volunteer to summarise The Grand High Witch's plot: to buy up sweet shops and sell children sweets and chocolates containing a magic formula which will turn them into mice as they go into school the next day, prompting their teachers to kill them with mousetraps.

Continue to the end of 'The Ancient Ones'. How has the danger that Boy is in increased? (Bruno Jenkins has been turned into a mouse, and now the narrator has been sniffed out, too.)

Read on through the next two chapters. Ask the children to note the detail of the metamorphosis, pausing to explain the meaning of the word: a change of form or a transformation. (The boys are turned physically into mice but retain their own minds and voices.)

'Hello, Grandmamma' to 'The Plan'

Read the next chapter at a fast pace. What is Boy's next mission? (To steal the potion to use it on the witches.) What makes the job so dangerous? (The Grand High Witch might return to her room at any minute.)

Read on to the start of 'The Plan'. Establish that Boy's next challenge is to get into the hotel kitchen and poison the witches' food. Pause to notice the 'hook' at the end of the chapter that makes us want to read on. (To find out whether Boy will succeed in his *big job*.)

'In the Kitchen' to the end

Continue quickly through the next three chapters. Discuss how the author sustains pace and tension with events unfolding quickly (the cook spotting Boy, the mouse chase, Mr Jenkins accosting Grandmamma, the formula working on the witches).

Read on to the end of the story. Then share reactions. Is it a surprising ending and, if so, why? (We wouldn't expect Boy to stay as a mouse.) In what way is the ending also a beginning? (This is just the start of the plan to rid the world of witches.)

Second reading

Re-reading the story should allow the children to explore it in more depth, focusing on plot construction, character portrayal, key themes and language.

Plot

Help the children to see how the plot can be divided roughly into three sections. The first

chapter through to the end of 'Summer Holidays' sets the scene, introduces characters and hints at future events, such as Boy encountering more witches. The second section, from 'The Meeting' to the end of 'Bruno', focuses on the problem that Boy and his grandmother face: how to stop the witches from carrying out their plan to rid England of all its children. The third section, from 'Hello, Grandmamma' to the final chapter, describes the resolution: how the intrepid pair foil the witches' plan and turn it back on them, then devise a way to continue ridding the world of the witches.

Character

Characters can be analysed in terms of fairytale heroes and villains. Discuss what makes Boy and his grandmother likeable. (Boy is a brave, stoical orphan; Grandmamma is kind, wise, caring and a fun companion.) What makes them unlikely or unusual heroes? (Boy is just a small boy who becomes a mouse; Grandmamma smokes cigars, is rebellious, tells fibs to Mr Stringer and the doctors.)

Focus on the witches as fairytale villains. Mention other fairytale characters like the giant in 'Jack and the Beanstalk', or the wolf in 'Little Red Riding Hood' and recall that they wanted to kill (and eat) children. Discuss what makes the Grand High Witch so hideous, encouraging The children to cite their favourite revolting details. Discuss the formula in terms of a fairytale potion, exploring how the recipe combines 'traditional' witches' brew ingredients with surreal ideas such as melted telescopes and alarm clocks.

Themes

Use questions to promote understanding of key themes. In what ways is the story a classic fairy tale? (The clearly delineated hero and villain characters – a small but virtuous hero outwitting a larger and more powerful, evil enemy). How is it a fairytale ending? (It is a happy ending as good triumphs over evil, and the heroes live happily, coming to terms with Boy's transformation.)

Guided reading

Focus on the central relationship between Boy and Grandmamma and ask the children what proves how strong their love is. (It makes no real difference to Grandmamma that her grandson has been turned into a mouse –she loves him as much as she did before. Boy is pleased that he will not outlive her, as he did his parents, and have to live alone.)

Style

As you re-read, encourage the children to look out for language features that they might recognise from other Roald Dahl stories. Highlight the use of capital letters or italics for emphasis or to suggest internal monologue; the idiosyncratic spellings used to convey The Grand High Witch's heavy accent; and the playful alliterations such as *frizzled like a fritter* and *cooked like a carrot*. Invite the children to identify invented words too (such as *frizzled* and *phizzing*). Note also changes of tempo, such as the rhyming verse used when The Grand High Witch gets excited by her own ideas at the meeting.

Encourage the children to think about the humour in the novel. Elicit the idea of black comedy and what we mean by that term: showing a funny side to something that is grotesque or gruesome or usually serious. Point out how humour undercuts what could be unhappy events. For example, when Bruno is transformed into a mouse, he still remains a greedy little character. Identify different elements in the novel that contribute to the humour: funny events (like mouse-Boy getting caught in the cook's trousers), funny ideas and words (clean children smelling like dogs' droppings to witches), and funny pictures, such as the row of bald witches in 'The Recipe' or Bruno changing into the mouse in 'Bruno Jenkins Disappears'.

Shared reading

Extract 1

● Read Extract 1. Circle *ghoul* and *barghest* and ask the children if they have heard of either. (A graveyard-dwelling phantom, and a monstrous dog-goblin.) Discuss the dark humour that comes from putting such supernatural content in the deadpan style of a non-chronological report.

● Revise onomatopoeia and alliteration in words such as *squish, squiggle* and *phwisst*, and note again that, although the author is describing terrible things (children being killed by witches), his playful use of language lightens the mood.

● Focus on the description of what happens when a child is caught. Identify a simile (*like a hunter stalking*) and discuss what it suggests (stealth, deadly intent). Examine sentence length, pointing out how the short, staccato sentences (*She treads softly. She moves quietly*) mimic the witch's careful, halting progress.

● Challenge the children to extend the sentence pattern beginning *Sparks fly. Flames leap…* (For example, *Owls shriek. Hair sizzles.*) What effect do these two-word sentences have? (They suggest sudden, explosive action.) Why are italic and capital letters used?

Extract 2

● Read Extract 2 and establish its main purpose: to help us visualise The Grand High Witch.

● Again look for similes or metaphors (*As though it had been pickled in vinegar; a look of serpents*).

● Challenge the children to find all the adjectives, and circle them as they go. Explore unfamiliar ones (such as *wizened, putrid, cankered*), seeing if the children can work out the meaning from the context and suggest words that could replace them.

● Continue to work through the adjectives, deciding which are purely descriptive and which are emotive. For example, *crumpled* is descriptive, *fearsome* and *ghastly* are emotive as they include an emotional comment.

● What difference does it make that the narrator tells us his reactions, for instance when he is shaken and nearly screams as he sees the face under the mask? (We share the experience with him, and feel his revulsion and horror.) Ask the children to pick out the words that describe his feelings or reactions: *transfixed, numbed, magnetized*.

Extract 3

● After reading this extract, ask what Boy has done. (Put the Mouse-Maker in the witches' soup.)

● Describe his mood at the start of the extract. (Triumphant, happy, exhilarated.) When and how does the tone change? (When he is spotted.) What is his mood after? (Frightened, desperate.)

● Focus on the hustle and bustle of the kitchen. Underline the present participles *bustling, steaming, spluttering, boiling*. Challenge the children to extend the sentence pattern with similar ideas, such as *soup was simmering, knives were chopping*.

● Consider sentence length again, this time underlining the long sentence *And I caught a glimpse…* Explore how it gives a detailed description through Boy's eyes of how swiftly and unexpectedly everything happens.

● Examine the passage starting *I hit the floor and jumped up…* Look for any verbs that are repeated in different forms (simple past tense and present participles): *dodged, dodging; swerved, swerving; twisted, twisting; turned, turning*. What effect do they have? (They evoke chaotic, fast and repeated movements.)

● Which lines help us to see the scene from a mouse's point of view? (*The whole floor seemed to be full of black boots stamping away at me.*)

Extract 1

A Note about Witches

A REAL WITCH gets the same pleasure from squelching a child as *you* get from eating a plateful of strawberries and thick cream.

She reckons on doing away with one child a week. Anything less than that and she becomes grumpy.

One child a week is fifty-two a year.
Squish them and squiggle them and make them disappear.
That is the motto of all witches.

Very carefully a victim is chosen. Then the witch stalks the wretched child like a hunter stalking a little bird in the forest. She treads softly. She moves quietly. She gets closer and closer. Then at last, when everything is ready… *phwisst!*… and she swoops! Sparks fly. Flames leap. Oil boils. Rats howl. Skin shrivels. And the child disappears.

A witch, you must understand, does not knock children on the head or stick knives into them or shoot at them with a pistol. People who do those things get caught by the police.

A witch never gets caught. Don't forget that she has magic in her fingers and devilry dancing in her blood. She can make stones jump about like frogs and she can make tongues of flame go flickering across the surface of the water.

These magic powers are very frightening.

Luckily, there are not a great number of REAL WITCHES in the world today. But there are still quite enough to make you nervous. In England, there are probably about one hundred of them altogether. Some countries have more, others have not quite so many. No country in the world is completely free from WITCHES.

A witch is always a woman.

I do not wish to speak badly about women. Most women are lovely. But the fact remains that all witches *are* women. There is no such thing as a male witch.

On the other hand, a ghoul is always a male. So indeed is a barghest. Both are dangerous. But neither of them is half as dangerous as a REAL WITCH.

Text © 1983, Roald Dahl Nominee Ltd.

Extract 2

Frizzled Like a Fritter

Very slowly, the young lady on the platform raised her hands to her face. I saw her gloved fingers unhooking something behind her ears, and then… then she caught hold of her cheeks and lifted her face clean away! The whole of that pretty face came away in her hands!

It was a mask!

As she took off the mask, she turned sideways and placed it carefully upon a small table near by, and when she turned round again and faced us, I very nearly screamed out loud.

That face of hers was the most frightful and frightening thing I have ever seen. Just looking at it gave me the shakes all over. It was so crumpled and wizened, so shrunken and shrivelled, it looked as though it had been pickled in vinegar. It was a fearsome and ghastly sight. There was something terribly wrong with it, something foul and putrid and decayed. It seemed quite literally to be rotting away at the edges, and in the middle of the face, around the mouth and cheeks, I could see the skin all cankered and worm-eaten, as though maggots were working away in there.

There are times when something is so frightful you become mesmerized by it and can't look away. I was like that now. I was transfixed. I was numbed. I was magnetized by the sheer horror of this woman's features. But there was more to it than that. There was a look of serpents in those eyes of hers as they flashed around the audience.

I knew immediately, of course, that this was none other than The Grand High Witch herself. I knew also why she had worn a mask. She could never have moved around in public, let alone book in at a hotel, with her real face. Everyone who saw her would have run away screaming.

Text © 1983, Roald Dahl Nominee Ltd.

Extract 3

In the Kitchen

I swung from the handle of one saucepan to the handle of another all the way along that top shelf, while far below me cooks and waiters were all bustling about and kettles were steaming and pans were spluttering and pots were boiling and I thought to myself, *Oh boy, this is the life! What fun it is to be a mouse and doing an exciting job like this!* I kept right on swinging. I swung most marvellously from handle to handle, and I was enjoying myself so much that I completely forgot I was in full view of anyone in the kitchen who might happen to glance upwards. What came next happened so quickly I had no time to save myself. I heard a man's voice yelling, 'A mouse! Look at that dirty little mouse!' And I caught a glimpse below me of a white-coated figure in a tall white hat and then there was a flash of steel as the carving-knife whizzed through the air and there was a shoot of pain in the end of my tail and suddenly I was falling and falling head-first towards the floor.

Even as I fell, I knew just what had happened. I knew that the tip of my tail had been cut off and that I was about to crash on to the floor and everyone in the kitchen would be after me. 'A mouse!' they were shouting. 'A mouse! A mouse! Catch it quick!' I hit the floor and jumped up and ran for my life. All around me there were big black boots going *stamp stamp stamp* and I dodged around them and ran and ran and ran, twisting and turning, and dodging and swerving across the kitchen floor. 'Get it!' they were shouting. 'Kill it! Stamp on it!' The whole floor seemed to be full of black boots stamping away at me and I dodged and swerved and twisted and turned and then in sheer desperation, hardly knowing what I was doing, wanting only a place to hide, I ran up the trouser-leg of one of the cooks and clung to his sock!

Plot, character and setting

SECTION
4

Consequences

> **Objective:** To use evidence from across a text to explain events or ideas.
> **What you need:** Copies of *The Witches*, flipchart, photocopiable page 15, scissors, glue, paper.

What to do

● Ask the children to consider all the important events that drive forward the plot of *The Witches* – events without which the storyline could not develop. Suggest that some are accidental or chance incidents, some deliberate acts. For example, it is in an accident that Boy's parents are killed and so he goes to live with his grandmother; and it is by chance that his grandmother falls ill so they end up holidaying in Bournemouth where the witches are holding their annual meeting. But it is a deliberate act that Boy steals the formula and puts it in the witches' soup, so

they are turned into mice. Write the children's suggestions of key plot incidents on the flipchart, dividing them under the two headings of 'Accidental' and 'Deliberate'.

● Hand out photocopiable page 15 and ask the children to cut out and match the events and consequences, then paste them down in the order they feature in the plot.

> **Differentiation**
> **For older/more confident learners:** Challenge the children to identify more key events and consequences and add them to the cut-and-paste sequence.
> **For younger/less confident learners:** Organise the children to work in pairs to complete the cut-and-paste activity, checking the order before sticking.

Cliffhangers

> **Objective:** To understand how writers use different structures to create coherence and impact.
> **What you need:** Copies of *The Witches*, individual whiteboards and pens.

What to do

● Focus on the cliffhangers in the story. Explain or revise the concept of a cliffhanger, where a chapter or episode in a story ends in such an exciting and tantalising way that we are left in suspense wanting eagerly to know what happens next.

● Challenge the children to identify a dramatic cliffhanger in *The Witches*. For example, at the end of 'Hello, Grandmamma', the cliffhanger question is: Can Boy steal the formula from The Grand High Witch's room before she returns?

● Ask the children to work in pairs to scan the novel for more cliffhangers, looking for short paragraphs or sentences that make us want to

read on to find out what happens next. The children should summarise them in note form on their whiteboards.

● When the pairs have finished, bring them back together to discuss as a class which of the cliffhangers work best, and how – for example, by building suspense or foreshadowing something that will happen later.

> **Differentiation**
> **For older/more confident learners:** Challenge the pairs to write brief chapter blurbs based on some of their cliffhangers, following the style of the cover blurb. (*Luckily one boy and his grandmother know how to recognize these vile creatures – but can they get rid of them for good?*)
> **For younger/less confident learners:** Provide the pairs with page references to help them locate significant cliffhangers.

PAGE
11

READ & RESPOND: Activities based on The Witches

Plot, character and setting

All about Norway

> **Objective:** To infer writers' perspectives from what is written and from what is implied.
> **What you need:** Copies of *The Witches*, flipchart, photocopiable page 16, writing materials.
> **Cross-curricular link:** Geography.

What to do

● Tell the children that they are going to focus on Norway as a setting for part of the novel. Remind them that Roald Dahl's parents were Norwegian and that he spent his summer holidays in Norway, as the boy in the story had done before his parents died.

● Hand out photocopiable page 16 and ask the children to work in pairs to scan the novel for the information needed to complete it.

● Afterwards, bring the class back together to share what has been found. Consider what part Norway plays as a setting in the novel. Reflect on the facts that the climate seems harsh in winter, the landscape is rugged or bleak, and Boy loses his parents while he is there. Ask the children how they think he feels about Norway nevertheless, and why. (He loves going there and is disappointed when he can't have the summer holidays there. He likes to hear his grandmother's stories about adventurous boat trips, fishing and shrimping, and eating mussels. When they return to Norway at the end of the book he says he has always loved brown Norwegian goats'-milk cheese.) Do the children think this reflects the author's own feelings about Norway?

> **Differentiation**
> **For older/more confident learners:** Challenge the pairs to research more about Norway to add to the photocopiable sheets.
> **For younger/less confident learners:** Provide chapter or page references to help the children locate information about Norway.

An unconventional grandmother

> **Objective:** To make notes on and use evidence from across a text to explain events or ideas.
> **What you need:** Copies of *The Witches*, flipchart, photocopiable page 17, writing materials.
> **Cross-curricular link:** PSHE.

What to do

● Explain to the children that, in this lesson, they are going to focus on the character of Grandmamma.

● Briefly share any details the children can recall about her, noting them on the flipchart. Encourage the children to think about what she looks like (old, wrinkled, fat, wears lace, for example) as well as her behaviour and characteristics (she enjoys smoking cigars, studying witches, storytelling; she is loving towards, and willing to give up everything for, her grandson).

● Ask the children to decide in which ways she is a stereotypical grandmother (such as her age and wrinkles) and in which ways she is unconventional or defies the stereotypes (for example, in smoking cigars).

● Organise the children into pairs to work on photocopiable page 17. Advise them to scan the book for details. They might be able to use direct quotes for the speech bubbles.

> **Differentiation**
> **For older/more confident learners:** Ask the pairs to list 'stereotypical' features about grandparents and discuss how far Boy's grandmother and their own grandparents (or older relatives) conform to them.
> **For younger/less confident learners:** Ask the pairs to talk about their own grandmothers (or other older relatives) and how they are conventional/unconventional.

Plot, character and setting

Storyboard

Objective: To identify how narrative texts are structured.
What you need: Copies of *The Witches*, flipchart, writing materials.
Cross-curricular links: Drama, art and design.

What to do

● Read the chapter 'The Mouse-Burglar'. What makes this an exciting episode in the novel? (It is full of tension and drama, as Boy must steal the formula to stop the witches' evil plan, but he risks being caught at any moment by The Grand High Witch.)
● Identify the main events that happen in the sequence, noting them in order on the flipchart.
● Now tell the children that they are going to imagine they are directing a film of this part of the story. Explain that film-makers often use a storyboard (a series of pictures showing the scene(s)) to plan a film sequence.
● Organise the children to work in pairs to scan the chapter and make notes and basic sketches for a storyboard of six to eight frames. Advise them that they should include brief but specific details of the characters, setting and action included in each scene.

Differentiation

For older/more confident learners: Encourage the pairs to suggest ways to make their film sequence exciting, for example, by adding music or sound effects.
For younger/less confident learners: Help the children to 'summarise' their scenes in labelled drawings for their storyboard.

Mouse-Boy

Objective: To understand underlying themes, causes and points of view.
What you need: Copies of *The Witches*, flipchart, photocopiable page 18, writing materials.
Cross-curricular links: Science, mathematics.

What to do

● Ask the children to summarise how Boy feels when he discovers he has been turned into a mouse. (He takes it in his stride and comes to rather enjoy the benefits it brings.) Are the children surprised by this response, and, if so, why? How would they react in his place?
● Challenge the children to list all the aspects of being a mouse that Boy thinks are positive (for example, being able to run fast and swing around from his tail; not having to go to school or take exams; having no money worries). Note these on the flipchart. Draw up a second column and ask the children to list all the negative things about being a mouse (the dangers of being attacked by a cat, trapped, poisoned, and so on). Go on to remind the children that a mouse's fast heartbeat means it will not live for very long. Does Boy see this as a positive or negative thing and why? (Positive, because he will not outlive his grandmother as he did his parents.)
● Hand out photocopiable page 18 and ask the children to work individually to fill it in. Advise them to think of qualities that Boy has when he is a person (for example, he is good at woodwork), qualities he acquires as a mouse (agility, fast movement), and qualities he has as a mouse-boy (those that remain for both 'states' of being, such as being a loving grandson).

Differentiation

For older/more confident learners: Challenge the children to consider another animal and list all the positive and negative aspects of being turned into one.
For younger/less confident learners: Provide pictures of a familiar animal and challenge the children to list positive and/or negative aspects of being one.

Plot, character and setting

A mouse's view

> **Objective:** To sustain engagement with longer texts, using different techniques to make the text come alive.
> **What you need:** Copies of *The Witches*, flipchart, individual whiteboards and pens.
> **Cross-curricular link:** Design and technology.

What to do

● Read the chapter 'The Heart of a Mouse'. Ask the children to list the adaptations and facilities Grandmamma provides at the house now Boy is a mouse, and what they are used for (for example, stepladders to climb onto tables and chairs; a silver sugar basin for a bath). Write suggestions on the flipchart.

● Arrange the children into small groups. Explain that they are going to think of more adaptations that would be useful for Boy now he is a mouse. They should begin by thinking of all the everyday objects he will need, such as a bed, a hairbrush, plates and bowls, and so on, and then, what other everyday objects could be used to make them.

● When the groups have had time to think of ideas, invite volunteers to present them to the class.

> **Differentiation**
> **For older/more confident learners:** Let the groups use ICT to develop a design brief for one of their adaptations.
> **For younger/less confident learners:** Let the groups list everyday objects that could be useful to a mouse-person, or sketch and label a design brief for one of their ideas.

The Jenkins' reunion

> **Objective:** To improvise using a range of drama strategies and conventions to explore themes such as hopes, fears, desires.
> **What you need:** Copies of *The Witches*, flipchart.
> **Cross-curricular link:** Drama.

What to do

● Read at pace the chapters 'Mr and Mrs Jenkins Meet Bruno', and 'Mr Jenkins and His Son'.

● Challenge the children to pick out any words or phrases that describe Mr and Mrs Jenkins (*coarse, rude, angry*) and to suggest other words of their own (loud, prim, standoffish, frightened). Write their ideas on the flipchart.

● Ask what more we learn about Bruno from the dialogue (he is always having mishaps, overeats, gets wind) and add notes to the flipchart. Expand this character sketch with any other information the children can recall about Bruno from earlier in the novel, for example, that he is greedy, cheeky and can be cruel.

● Organise groups of three and explain that they are going to improvise a scene in which Bruno is reunited, as a mouse, with his parents. Advise the children to think how he would describe what has happened to him and how each character is feeling. (Mrs Jenkins, terrified and upset; Mr Jenkins, furious; Bruno, worried about Topsy the cat, but probably more interested in the benefits of being a mouse, such as not going to school.)

● Allow time for the improvisations, then invite one or two groups to perform their scenes for the class.

> **Differentiation**
> **For older/more confident learners:** Challenge the groups to adapt their scenes for a stage play or film script of the book.
> **For younger/less confident learners:** Discuss ideas for dialogue in more detail, for example, rehearsing step-by-step what happened to Bruno.

Plot, character and setting

Consequences

● Decide which consequence follows which event. Then cut and paste them in the order they happen.

Event	Consequence
A witch smells out Boy.	Boy goes to live with his grandmother.
Mouse-Boy is spotted in the kitchen.	Boy encounters his first witch.
A chambermaid discovers Boy's pet mice.	Boy is turned into a mouse.
Boy's parents are killed in a car crash.	Boy loses his mouse tail.
Boy works on the roof of his tree-house.	Boy comes to overhear The Grand High Witch's plan.

Plot, character and setting

All about Norway

● Write down any facts about Norway that we learn from *The Witches*.

Describe the features of the landscape.	
What is the climate like?	
Describe Norwegian food.	
What holiday activities do people enjoy?	
Name some places in Norway.	

SCHOLASTIC
www.scholastic.co.uk
READ & RESPOND: Activities based on The Witches

Plot, character and setting

An unconventional grandmother

● Write down three things about Grandmamma that are 'typical' of grandmothers.

1. _____

2. _____

3. _____

● Write down three things about Grandmamma that make her an unusual grandmother.

1. _____

2. _____

3. _____

● What are Grandmamma's views on:

1. Children and baths? _____

_____

2. Children smoking? _____

_____

3. Doctors' advice? _____

_____

Illustration © 1983, Quentin Blake.

Mouse-Boy

- Use the diagram to note down words and phrases that could describe Boy before and after his transformation. Do some words fit in both circles?

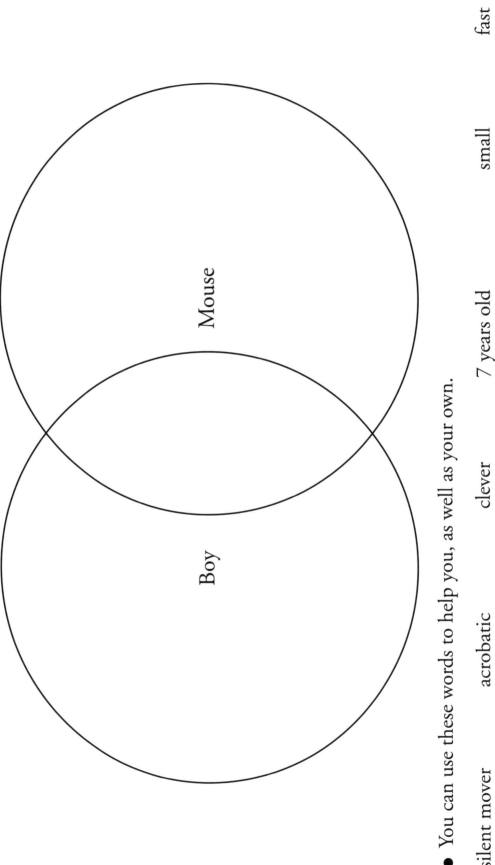

Mouse

Boy

- You can use these words to help you, as well as your own.

silent mover   acrobatic   clever   7 years old   small   fast

loving grandson   quick-witted   skilled in woodwork   agile

SCHOLASTIC
www.scholastic.co.uk

Talk about it

Exciting episodes

Objective: To present a spoken argument, sequencing points logically, defending views with evidence.
What you need: Copies of *The Witches*, flipchart, photocopiable page 22, writing materials.

What to do

● Ask the children to consider pace in the story. Which episodes are slower and more reflective? (For example, Grandmamma telling stories about witches.) Which are fast, tense and exciting? (Scenes such as when mouse-Boy is spotted in the kitchen.) Invite the children to talk about their favourite parts of the story.
● Hand out photocopiable page 22 and give the children time to choose and think about one of the episodes or suggest another one. Let them make brief, key-word notes.

● Then, invite volunteers to explain why they chose their episode. Prompt them to analyse what makes it exciting.
● After everyone has spoken, note the author's techniques on the flipchart. They might be, for example: details or dialogue that make characters or situations frightening; fast-paced action, perhaps given in short sentences with strong active verbs; implied risks or dangers.

Differentiation
For older/more confident learners: Let the children work in small groups to create a new episode for a *The Witches* sequel.
For younger/less confident learners: Ask the children to discuss in small groups which parts of the story they like best.

A mouse's voice

Objective: To use different narrative techniques to engage and entertain the reader.
What you need: Copies of *The Witches*, flipchart.

What to do

● Read the first paragraph of the second chapter and ask the children who is speaking. (Boy, or mouse-Boy after his transformation.) What are the two encounters referred to? (When he meets his first witch while in a tree, and when he sees the witches at the hotel.)
● Explain that every story has a 'narrative voice': the person who is telling it. Some can be, like this story, in the first person, others in the third person. Write two lines on the flipchart to make this clear:

● *I crouched behind the screen and peered through the crack.* (first person)
● *He crouched behind the screen and peered through the crack.* (third person)

● Can the children suggest why the author chose to tell this story in the first person? (Perhaps to make it convincing and believable; to make it

more personal, immediate and involving; to help us understand Boy's feelings and reactions.)
● Organise the children into pairs. Tell them to choose a paragraph from 'The Kitchen' to rehearse orally, changing it into the third person. Model a line or two on the flipchart:

● *I was on my own now. I stood clasping the little bottle.*
● *He was on his own now. He stood clasping the little bottle.*

● After preparation time, invite volunteers to read out their paragraphs. Ask the audience how this changes the text for the reader. Suggest that using the first person might help us to appreciate better how Boy feels about becoming a mouse, and also gives the story a 'true tale' feel because it is told in a similar way to a memoir or autobiography.

Differentiation
For older/more confident learners: Let the pairs choose another paragraph from anywhere in the novel.
For younger/less confident learners: Suggest paragraphs to alter, and model the first lines.

Talk about it

Witch in the hot seat

Objective: To develop drama techniques to explore in role a variety of situations or respond to stimuli.
What you need: Copies of *The Witches*, flipchart, individual whiteboards and pens.

What to do

● Tell the children that they are going to hot-seat The Grand High Witch and challenge her about herself, her life and her opinions.
● Begin by re-reading 'Frizzled Like a Fritter' and 'Formula 86…'. As you read, remind the children that The Grand High Witch is speaking English as a foreign language. Highlight some of her speech mannerisms: the way she rolls her Rs and pronounces W as V; her use of rhyme and alliteration; her incorrect use of the present continuous tense; and occasional omission of the definite article *the*, for example, *Child is starting to grow fur.*
● Choose a confident child to play The Grand High Witch, and advise him or her to prepare by scanning the text for thoughts, opinions and speech idiosyncrasies. Arrange the rest of the class into small groups and give them time to note down questions they would like to ask The Grand High Witch.
● Put The Grand High Witch in the hot seat, inviting children from each group to question her.
● When all the groups have asked their questions, explore which were most revealing and why. Has anything new or surprising been uncovered? What drives her and makes her so villainous?

Differentiation
For older/more confident learners: The children could enact a trial, appointing a judge, jury and lawyers, and accuse the Witch of conspiracy to kill all the children of England.
For younger/less confident learners: Before the groups begin, think together of some questions to ask the Witch.

Formula 86

Objective: To explore how writers use language for comic and dramatic effects.
What you need: Copies of *The Witches*, photocopiable page 23, writing materials.
Cross-curricular link: Science.

What to do

● Tell the children they are going to focus on the recipe for the Mouse-Maker formula.
● Organise pairs and hand out photocopiable page 23. Tell the children to scan 'The Recipe' in order to fill in the recipe details. Before they begin, briefly revise the key features of instruction texts, such as the use of imperative verbs and lists of what you need and what to do.
● When the children have finished, invite them to explore the ingredients – its combination of 'traditional' witches' foodstuffs (mouse tails, frogs' juice, tongues and claws) with bizarre 'modern' items such as boiled telescopes and roasted alarm clocks.
● Speculate on what the imaginary creatures might be. What do the children think a gruntle or a catspringer might be like? Encourage them to cite clues from the text, for example, a gruntle lays eggs and builds nests, a catspringer lives in a burrow. What real creatures lay eggs in nests? (Birds and reptiles.) What kinds of animals live in burrows? (Rodents and rabbits.)

Differentiation
For older/more confident learners: Challenge pairs to flesh out details for one of the imaginary creatures, such as its diet, habitat, behaviour, and so on.
For younger/less confident learners: Ask the pairs to choose one imaginary creature to talk about, then draw and label it.

Talk about it

Unanswered questions

Objective: To read between the lines and find evidence for their interpretation.
What you need: Copies of *The Witches*, flipchart, photocopiable page 24, writing materials.

What to do

● Tell the children that they are going to think about questions or points that are raised in the story but remain unanswered. For example: Why is Grandmamma's thumb missing and what is it she can't speak about? Who were/are the three frogs in The Grand High Witch's bedroom?
● Hand out photocopiable page 24. Ask the children to work in pairs to discuss ideas and fill in the sheets.
● Bring the class back together. Invite the pairs to share their ideas, and discuss which work best and why. This should take into account how well the ideas keep with the style and content of the novel. For example, the frogs are likely to be children (The Grand High Witch's main target), and Grandmamma might well have lost her thumb in an incident similar to the frizzling episode.
● Choose a few of the best ideas and, as a shared activity, develop them for possible plot lines, noting key characters and events on the flipchart.

Differentiation
For older/more confident learners: Ask pairs to discuss how they would develop the plot further for each scenario.
For younger/less confident learners: Consider possible scenarios together before pairs attempt the photocopiable sheet.

The Witches: a sequel

Objective: To use a range of oral techniques to present persuasive arguments and engaging narratives.
What you need: Copies of *The Witches*, flipchart, individual whiteboards and pens.

What to do

● Ask the children if they can explain what a sequel is and give you examples (to books or films). Explain that they are going to plan a sequel to *The Witches*.
● Begin by reading the last chapter. Discuss how the novel closes with a sense of another beginning rather than just an ending (all the work that lies ahead for Boy and his grandmother in ridding the world of witches).
● Challenge the children to pick out the main stages in the heroes' plan. For example:
  ● Produce more Mouse-Maker formula.
  ● Sneak into the castle and put the formula in the witches' food.
  ● Take cats to the castle to catch and kill the mouse-witches.
  ● Move into the castle to find the details of all the other witches in the world.
● Organise small groups and explain that the plot of their sequel will be based on these events. Advise the children to think of some twists and turns in the plot to make it exciting and gripping. For example, mouse-Boy could get caught by the new Grand High Witch, or one of the cats starts chasing him. They should note their ideas on their whiteboards.
● When the children have had discussion time, encourage volunteers from each group to summarise their plots to the class.
● Encourage constructive feedback and positive criticism.

Differentiation
For older/more confident learners: Encourage the groups to consider characters in more detail, drawing up a cast list.
For younger/less confident learners: Talk about some events and plot lines together to get the children started.

Talk about it

Exciting episodes

- Choose a favourite episode from below and add another one of your own.
- Make short notes so that you can explain what makes it exciting.

Boy is in a tree. A witch is right below him.

The Grand High Witch returns when mouse-Boy is hiding in her room.

Mouse-Boy is spotted in the hotel kitchen.

Boy sees a witch getting frizzled.

A witch sniffs out Boy behind the screen.

Another episode:

Formula 86

● Write the recipe for Formula 86 Delayed Action Mouse-Maker.

Ingredients	Equipment

Method

1. _____

2. _____

3. _____

4. _____

5. _____

Illustrations © 1983, Quentin Blake.

Talk about it

Unanswered questions

● Suggest an answer to each of these questions raised in the story.

1. What happened to Grandmamma that she cannot talk about?

2. How did she lose her thumb?

3. Who were/are the frogs in The Grand High Witch's hotel room?

4. Who is the new Grand High Witch and where was she found?

5. What happens when Bruno arrives home with his parents?

Illustrations© 1983, Quentin Blake.

Get writing

Grandmamma's diary

> **Objective:** To experiment with different narrative form and styles to write their own stories.
> **What you need:** Copies of *The Witches*, writing materials.

What to do
- Tell the children that, in this lesson, they are going to write an entry for Grandmamma's diary during the time that she was an active *witchophile*.
- Ask what you know about Grandmamma's past in connection with witches. (She had a terrifying encounter with a witch when she was a little girl; she somehow lost her thumb; she used to travel around the world trying to find The Grand High Witch's headquarters.)
- Ask the children to think about what to put in Grandmamma's diary. They might like to write as a little girl after meeting the witch, or the incident when she lost her thumb, or a narrow escape she might have had when trying to track down The Grand High Witch.
- Briefly recap a diary's layout and style points (date and location; first person, chronological, informal, chatty, personal, revelatory; could be in note form), and give the children time to draft their diary entries.
- Invite volunteers to read their entries to the class, and encourage constructive feedback.

> **Differentiation**
> **For older/more confident learners:** Challenge the children to write another entry by the older Grandmamma, based on a day in the novel.
> **For younger/less confident learners:** Let the children work in pairs to discuss and draft their diary entries.

Missing children

> **Objective:** To use different narrative techniques to engage and entertain the reader.
> **What you need:** Copies of *The Witches*, flipchart, individual whiteboards and pens.

What to do
- Read 'My Grandmother' from *We were in the big living-room*, to the end of the chapter.
- Draw and label three columns on the flipchart with the headings 'Missing child', 'Location' and 'Metamorphosis'. Revise the meaning of *metamorphosis* if necessary.
- Invite the children to scan the chapter and pick out relevant information to help you fill in the columns for each missing child.
- Then organise the children into pairs and challenge them to invent another child, location and metamorphosis. Get them started by modelling one or two ideas. For example:
  - Missing child: Boris.
  - Location: A pharmacy on a street in Oslo.
  - Metamorphosis: He is found shrunken and trapped inside a glass medicine jar; the stopper can't seem to be removed.
- Allow the children time to think through and discuss their ideas, writing them under the relevant headings on their whiteboards.
- Then encourage the pairs to share their creations with the class. Add the best ideas to the columns on the flipchart.

> **Differentiation**
> **For older/more confident learners:** The children could think of more details and add more columns to the chart.
> **For younger/less confident learners:** Model ideas for the children before they begin, or prompt them with suggestions for locations or metamorphoses.

Get writing

How to spot a witch

> **Objective:** To make notes on and use evidence from across a text to explain events or ideas.
> **What you need:** Copies of *The Witches*, flipchart, photocopiable page 28, writing materials.

What to do

● Challenge the children to recall, without looking at the novel, some key facts that Grandmamma suggests would help someone to spot a witch. (They always wear gloves; they have large nose holes…) Can the children remember how Boy uses this information when he has his first encounters with witches? (The first time, he notices the woman is wearing gloves; the second time, he spots gloves and wigs.)

● Hand out photocopiable page 28 to pairs of children. Explain that they should scan the chapter 'How to Recognize a Witch' and extract and summarise facts to complete the sheets.

● Challenge the pairs to invent an extra fact that could be included in a witch-spotter's guide, for example, foods they enjoy or the sound they make when they snore.

● Afterwards, bring the class together to review the witch-spotter facts.

> **Differentiation**
> **For older/more confident learners:** Challenge the pairs to invent more facts to add to each section of the photocopiable sheet.
> **For younger/less confident learners:** Let the children choose one section from the photocopiable sheet and invent another fact to add to it.

The Grand High Witch:
an interview

> **Objective:** To devise and present scripted pieces, which maintain the attention of an audience, and evaluate the presentations.
> **What you need:** Copies of *The Witches*, flipchart, individual whiteboards and pens.
> **Cross-curricular link:** Drama.

What to do

● Tell the children that you want them to write a script for a television interview with The Grand High Witch.

● They will need to re-examine The Grand High Witch's manner of speaking, so that they are able to parody it in their script. (Briefly explain or revise the concept of parody.)

● Read 'Frizzled Like a Fritter' from *Her voice, I noticed* to the end of the following chapter. As you read, encourage the children to pick out words that describe how the Witch speaks, or identify her mannerisms. For example:

  ● sounds are harsh, guttural, rasping, grating, metallic, snarling, shrieking, growling;
  ● uses the present continuous tense (for past and simple present), such as *I am having my breakfast this morning*;
  ● Ws pronounced like Vs; Vs pronounced like Fs; rolls Rs; stresses Es;
  ● sometimes speaks in rhyme.

● Explore terms like *guttural* and *metallic*. Encourage children to read some lines to demonstrate how they think The Grand High Witch sounds.

● In pairs, tell the children to draft five questions, then write what they think The Grand High Witch would say in reply.

● Invite pairs to read their scripts to the class. Evaluate the interviews together.

> **Differentiation**
> **For older/more confident learners:** Let the children try to draft one interview answer as a rhyme in the manner of the Witch.
> **For younger/less confident learners:** Help the children to prepare by modelling in role a question and its answer.

Get writing

Formula 86: the antidote

> **Objective:** To adapt non-narrative forms and styles
> to write fiction or factual texts including poems.
> **What you need:** Copies of *The Witches*, flipchart,
> photocopiable page 29, writing materials.
> **Cross-curricular link:** Science.

What to do

● Tell the children that they are going to invent
their own recipe for an antidote to the Mouse-
Maker Formula that could turn Boy and
Bruno back into boys. Ensure that the children
understand what an antidote is: a medicine or
remedy for counteracting the effects of a poison
or disease.

● Organise the class in pairs and hand out
photocopiable page 29. Before the children begin,
review their work from the lesson 'Formula 86'.
Encourage them to analyse the ingredients: mouse
tails because it is for mouse metamorphosis;
telescopes to make children shrink, and so on.

● Using that recipe as a model, pose some
prompt questions to get the children thinking of

ingredients they could use. For example, *What
might turn a mouse into a boy?* ('Boyish' things
like a toy car or football boots?) *What might
make mouse-boys grow bigger again?* (Stirring in a
magnifying glass?)

● Share some ideas for the transformation stages.
For example, 'First he will feel a tingle. Then his
tail will shrivel and his whiskers wither…'

● Give the children time to complete the sheets,
then encourage the pairs to share their ideas with
the class.

> **Differentiation**
> **For older/more confident learners:** Challenge pairs
> to expand their description of the transformation
> process on the other side of the photocopiable sheet.
> **For younger/less confident learners:** Work together
> to suggest more ideas for ingredients or equipment, or
> ask more direct question prompts, such as *What could
> you use to make something grow larger?*

Hotel drama

> **Objective:** To vary the pace and develop the
> viewpoint through the use of direct and reported
> speech, portrayal of action, selection of detail.
> **What you need:** Copies of *The Witches*,
> photocopiable page 30, writing materials.
> **Cross-curricular link:** Citizenship.

What to do

● Read 'The Triumph' as far as *clapping and
cheering and laughing like mad.*

● Ask the children to imagine they are a news
reporter who was dining at the hotel when the
drama occurred. They are going to plan a front-
page news story describing what happened and
quoting interviews with witnesses.

● Remind the children that the witches

were supposedly at the hotel for an RSPCC
convention. Might the reporter see their sudden
vanishing as sinister? Might the hotel or its food
be under suspicion? How would the journalist
describe how the other guests and hotel staff
were affected?

● Hand out photocopiable page 30 and give the
children time to plan their news reports.

> **Differentiation**
> **For older/more confident learners:** Ask the children
> to use ICT to begin 'publishing' their front page.
> **For younger/less confident learners:** Ask
> the children to work in pairs to complete the
> photocopiable sheets.

How to spot a witch

● Complete this handy witch-spotter's guide.

| Physical features | Typical clothing  |

Behaviour and habits

Special powers

Other pointers and warnings

■SCHOLASTIC
www.scholastic.co.uk

$\mathcal{G}$et writing

Formula 86: the antidote

- Develop a potion to reverse the effects of Formula 86.
- List the ingredients and what they will do.

Ingredients	Effect it will have

What equipment and utensils will you need?

Explain how to make the antidote.

1. _____

2. _____

3. _____

4. _____

How will the antidote look when it is ready?

What will happen if Boy and Bruno take the antidote?

First _____

Next _____

Then _____

Finally _____

Hotel drama

● You are the lead journalist for the *Bournemouth Echo*. Plan the front-page story of the dramatic events in the Dining Room at the Hotel Magnificent.

The Bournemouth Echo

Headline

Photograph

Story summary

Caption

Quotes from three witnesses

Assessment

Assessment advice

In studying *The Witches*, children carry out a range of activities to exercise their speaking, listening, reading and writing skills. Assessment should be an ongoing process, recording progress and highlighting areas that need improvement. It should be based on contributions in shared work, as part of the whole class, as well as on written individual, paired and group work.

Begin each lesson by explaining its aim and, where possible, relate such objectives to other literacy and cross-curricular work. At the end of the lesson, encourage the children to assess their own work against the objective, and to decide which areas need further practice. Also encourage the children to provide constructive feedback for writing partners and groups.

Children could also create their own assessment activities, for example, working in groups to devise multiple choice or 'true or false' quizzes about the novel. They might compile spelling tests based on themes or topics (such as witches, the formula recipe, Norway) or parts of speech (verbs, nouns, adjectives, adverbs). They could devise cloze activities using The Grand High Witch's rhymes, or compile glossaries defining invented and unusual words from the novel.

Photocopiable page 32 is useful for assessment as it invites the children to compare *The Witches* with another book by Roald Dahl, examining common themes and literary features.

Recurring themes

> **Objective:** To understand how writers use different structures to create coherence and impact.
> **What you need:** Copies of *The Witches* and other familiar Dahl books, flipchart, photocopiable page 32, writing materials, DVD of *The Witches*, David Wood's playscript adaptation (also in Puffin) – optional.

What to do
● Encourage the children to tell you whether or not they enjoyed *The Witches* and why. Discuss their favourite parts of the story. Which parts are most memorable and why? What made them want to read on?
● Discuss the main events and key themes (a 'small-fry' hero outwitting a powerful and evil villain; the close bond between a boy and his grandmother; the power of love to transcend all barriers, even transformation into a mouse). Talk about how the themes are fed into the plot, characters and use of settings.

● If possible, watch the film version of *The Witches*. Talk about how 'faithful' it is to the original story and how successful the children think it is as an adaptation. What do they like or dislike about the treatment? If there is time, the class could go on to read, and even perform, David Wood's play, and discuss the way the novel has been adapted as dialogue and stage action.
● Ask the children to tell you about other books they have read by Roald Dahl. Can they suggest any aspects of *The Witches* that are characteristic of his writing (humour, invented words, horrible villains, vulnerable but brave child heroes)? Write suggestions on the flipchart.
● Let the children choose another Dahl book they have read (or suggest one that the class has read together) and provide copies, along with photocopiable page 32. Ask the children to consider the two books together, exploring in more detail any themes, plot or character types and style or language features that they share.

Recurring themes

● Review *The Witches* and another book by Roald Dahl.

Title	*The Witches*	
Central character(s) and hero(es)		
Villain(s)		
Most exciting or tense episode		
Funniest event or idea		
Unusual and/or invented words